Table of Contents

Preparing the
Children

Information and Ideas for Families Facing Serious Illness and Death

~Revised Edition~

By Kathy Nussbaum, RN, MS, APRN

ISBN 978-0-9847009-0-5

Book design: Ted Nussbaum
Cover design: Krista Nussbaum
Editors: Leslie Leyland Fields, Heather Barrett
Photography: Kathy Nussbaum

Other photographers:

Addrienne Comaduran	[pages 9 bottom, 12 top, 21 top, 37]
Arne Grisham	[page 41 bottom]
Isa Jennings	[page 69 top]
Jennifer King	[pages 67 bottom, 73 bottom]
Katy King	[page 82]
Melody Livingston	[front cover, pages 8 top, 25 bottom, 36]
Stephanie Randall	[page 22 bottom]
Abby Reed	[pages v, 29 bottom, 61 top]
Austin Reed	[page 62 top]
Mike Rostad	[page 60 top]
Jessica Skonberg	[pages 23 bottom, 61 bottom]
Stan Thompson	[page 13 top]
Sam Towarak	[title page, page 29 top]
Nolan Voth	[page 63 top]
Dave Wukasch	[pages 3 bottom, 4 bottom, 14 top, 21 bottom, 24 right]
Starla Voth	[pages 2 top, 4 top, 16 top, 23 top, 34 top, 47 top, 50 bottom, 55 top, 56 bottom, 62 bottom, 72 top]

Children's artwork:
Courageous Kids participants: Eugene, Oregon
Youth from Kodiak, Alaska and Lynden, Washington

ii

Introduction

It's difficult to know how to prepare for a journey of serious illness. The fear of death often tempts us to focus exclusively on a cure rather than preparing our families for the possibility of death. It seems easier to avoid the subject rather than face some difficult and emotional conversations. Young parents may be especially prone to avoiding the subject of death as they fight desperately to get well and to protect their children from emotional pain. They often feel they are "giving up" if they even discuss the possibility of death.

However, most children cope much better with painful experiences if they are given honest information and preparation rather than protection from the pain.

Preparing the Children was written by Kathy Nussbaum, a mental health nurse practitioner who has worked with hundreds of families facing life-threatening illness and death over the past 22 years. She has walked the path with many parents and grandparents who have struggled with a life-threatening illness and fears about preparing their children.

She has also walked with hundreds of children who have experienced the serious illness and death of a parent or grandparent, and she has repeatedly heard their pain and resentment regarding ways in which information and preparation were withheld from them.

Please continue reading this book regardless of your family member's prognosis at this point. Your children will benefit from the information provided whether the illness is cured or your family is forced to face the end of your loved one's life.

What Children Need During a Serious Illness

The news that your loved one has an illness that may not be curable will likely feel unreal and difficult to grasp. You may not even be able to say the word "die," much less discuss death in relation to *your* family. You may feel so overwhelmed, so fearful about what's to come, or so worried about crying in front of your children, that it may seem easier to avoid talking to them about the news.

However, children of all ages have the ability to figure out very quickly that something is wrong when parents get the news of a life-threatening illness. Your face and your behaviors will tell them you are upset; they just won't know why. This will create fear and anxiety in your children, even if they don't show it.

Young children will begin imagining explanations for your behavior, often creating fearful images in their mind. They may even think they are somehow responsible for the increased stress.

Older children will feel they are mature enough to handle news of any kind and may become resentful for many years if they aren't given honest information from the beginning.

So what do children need?
>They need honest information.
>They need to feel safe.
>They need to be included.
>They need to express their grief.

Children Need Honest Information

Although it may seem natural to protect children from painful information about life-limiting illness and death, most children cope much better if they are given honest information from the beginning. When we avoid giving information to children, it is usually because *we* are the ones who feel uncomfortable talking about the subject, not because our children will be unable to cope with it.

When giving children information, remember that their understanding of death will be different at various ages. The following age groups are approximate since children vary greatly in their rate of development.

How Children Understand Death

Age 0-2

Infants and toddlers do not have concepts for death or the future. Giving them information is not as important as meeting their physical needs and providing safety and comfort.

Age 2-6

At this age, children are beginning to have a concept of death. They step on bugs and play pretend games with weapons, but their level of understanding about the world may still make it difficult for them to comprehend death.

First, they may have confusion about what is alive and what is not alive. To them, cars or toys could be alive.

Second, they may have difficulty understanding *why* things happen. They believe in magical thinking and may think they've caused their loved person's illness by their behavior, actions, thoughts or wishes.

Third, they are often unable to grasp the concept that death is permanent. Even if they're told that death will be forever, they may interpret "forever" as being slightly longer than Mom or Dad's last business trip.

Young children are curious about changes they see happening. If they aren't given enough information, they will make up explanations that are based on fantasy. It is very important to give children of this age simple but factual information.

3

Ages 7-11

By this age children can grasp that death is permanent. They generally understand it is caused by something beyond themselves, although there still may be some magical thinking among the younger ones.

They often begin expressing concern and anxiety related to their own death, but they still may not fully understand abstract concepts like heaven.

The body becomes a focus for children of this age. They may be particularly disturbed by physical changes they see happening to their loved person, or they may begin looking for changes in their own bodies.

Teens

Teenagers have a full comprehension of death. They understand that death is irreversible and they are able to understand the basics of terminal disease processes. They can grasp abstract ideas related to death, and they tend to shut out thoughts of their own death.

Information About the Illness

Start by giving children simple explanations. They, like you, may need time to absorb small pieces of information before learning more.

"Most sicknesses go away when people take care of themselves or use the right medicine, but mom has a sickness that may not go away no matter what she does. She is very, very, very sick and the doctor says she is probably going to die. "

Talk about how the life-limiting illness differs from other illnesses or young children may assume other common illnesses can also lead to death.

Discuss whether or not the illness is communicable and how it is spread. Children often think they can catch a life-threatening illness by touching the person who is sick.

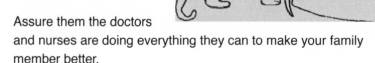

Explain that the illness was not caused by anything they did, said or thought.

Assure them the doctors and nurses are doing everything they can to make your family member better.

Tell children what you expect to happen in the following weeks and months or they may think that death could happen at any moment.

Be prepared for young children to review information again and again as they try to grasp it. They often do this by bringing it up to others in their lives. *"My dad is sick and he's going to die."* This can sound a bit shocking but it is normal and should be allowed.

Although children will be scared, they will also be curious about various things. Invite them to ask questions of any kind so they can get as much information as they need, but not so much that they get confused.

Older children will naturally want and need more detailed information. Sharing your thoughts and feelings freely will give them permission to talk openly about their own questions and concerns.

Assure them you will give them medical updates as you get them. This will build their trust, and they won't need to worry that things are happening that nobody is telling them.

Information About Normal Reactions

Kids often feel afraid when they see adults crying. Let them know it is good for adults to cry when they are sad and assure children they don't need to worry or try to make the tears stop [See Recommended Resources – *Tough Boris*].

Children and adults each have their own unique way of reacting to painful news. Some will cry; others won't. Some will want to talk about their feelings; others will be quiet and reflective. Some older children will want to be around the house; others will want to distance themselves from the family. All of these are normal reactions.

One thing that is very common during a serious illness is an increase in irritability; adults and children get more grumpy and impatient with each other. When this happens, acknowledge that it's normal and discuss ways to decrease the family stress.

Information About Death

It may feel like talking about death means giving up hope. Your family has undoubtedly been hoping or praying for a miracle and talking about death can make people feel they don't have enough faith.

However, preparing for a death does not require the loss of faith or hope. Many families have missed out on the opportunity to share meaningful and healing conversations with their loved ones because they counted on a physical miracle until it was too late.

A wise and godly patient once said,

"Prepare to die - prefer to live."

Use the word "die" as you explain death to your children. Other substitute words or phrases ("pass away," "pass on," etc.) may seem easier to say but they can cause unnecessary confusion for children.

Keep in mind that if your children watch television, they may have some rather distorted ideas about death. Talk about the differences between real death and TV deaths.

Ideas: Giving Information About Death

• Look outside and around your house for examples of death: a flower, a bird, or any form of life that could teach children about the life cycle.

• Ask a friend to go to a library or bookstore to get some books about death. Books provide a wonderful way to approach the subject of death and they allow time for children to review their content again and again [see Recommended Resources].

• Keep a record of funny or insightful things your children say or do. When they grow older, they will be curious about how they felt and acted during this time.

Children Need to Feel Safe

Children generally feel safe when their life is ordered and predictable and when they are surrounded by nurturing friends and family. During a serious family illness a child's world can become very insecure as they wonder what will come next and who will take care of them.

Keeping a child's life orderly and predictable usually involves maintaining daily routines and rules.

Normal Schedule

Although adults often have a new daily schedule when caring for a seriously ill family member, children should not be expected to do this. Rather, they should be encouraged to continue many of their normal activities.

 Ideas: Maintaining a Normal Schedule

- Don't pull the children out of extracurricular activities. Ask a friend to help with transportation if it's a problem for you.

- Try to have regular meals that include nutritious foods. The kids will be hungry even if you aren't, and it's very easy to let them snack on junk food when your routine is interrupted.

- Don't expect children to sit at the bedside of the ill family member for long periods of time. Most are not capable of this. Let them play with their friends and do their usual activities.

- Keep a regular bedtime that isn't too late. Children need plenty of sleep during this time.

Setting Limits

When families are experiencing a serious illness, it is common for children to have increased behavior problems.

It is also common for parents to decrease their normal discipline practices because of the extra strain on their energies.
Often, too, parents feel that children should be given some slack about the rules due to the situation.

However, even though it may seem unreasonable to be strict about discipline during this time, children actually feel more secure and can cope with family changes better when they have limits that are consistent and predictable.

If you are still having difficulty setting limits for your children, make a new plan that requires less of your energy.

Keep in mind that in order for a limit-setting plan to work, rules must be clear, and consequences should be small but consistent.

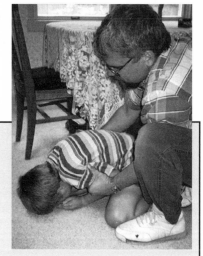

 Idea: Setting Limits

1. Discuss the importance of rules at your house and emphasize the most significant ones.

   Examples:
   No hurting others or their belongings.
   Follow directions the first time you're asked.
   Talk with respect [no put downs or talking back].

2. Acknowledge that rule breaking is often a result of increased anger, stress or frustration. Discuss ways of letting off steam without breaking rules.

3. Keep a point chart with two kinds of points: poor choices and good choices. When your child acts inappropriately or breaks a rule, calmly ask him/her to mark a poor choice point on the chart. When you see a positive behavior, ask him/her to mark a good choice point on the chart.

   At the end of the day, tally the points to see if the child owes you (more poor choice points) or you owe the child (more good choice points). Each point could be worth computer time, extra time before bed, time doing chores, etc.

4. Certain types of rule breaking may require immediate consequences such as 5-10 minute work chores.

Nurturing Support

Children of all ages need support and attention throughout the illness. They need to know that the ill family member is not the only person in the family worthy of the family's time and energy.

It is common for parents to be experiencing so much stress or personal grief during a serious illness that they are unable to be available to their children as usual.

No one can meet both their loved one's needs and their children's needs by themselves. Allow friends and family to help.

Keep in mind that parents may not be the primary support system for adolescents. Teens often feel their friends are their most valued supporters.

Ideas: Nurturing Support

• Find ways to give extra physical attention: invite the children to snuggle in ways you both enjoy, rub their backs, wrestle on the floor or brush their hair.

• Make a date with each child to do something you both enjoy. Go for a walk, a bike ride or a drive in the car to simply be together. Don't ignore the subject of the life-threatening illness but don't spend the whole time talking about it either.

• Remember to show an interest in things that happen in the children's daily lives, even if they seem insignificant compared to the illness.

• Lie down close to the children at bedtime. When it's quiet and the lights are out, they may feel safe enough to share their thoughts and concerns with you.

• Get support for yourself! Your children will feel safer knowing they are not responsible for meeting your emotional needs.

• If the children start getting lost in a stream of visitors, limit the number of guests. If this is too difficult, ask a trusted friend or family member to be in charge of your visitor schedule.

Infants and Toddlers

Although infants and toddlers are not old enough to understand serious illness and death, they are certainly old enough to be affected by them. Disruptions in their normal routine or interactions can be quite disturbing. They may tell you this with changes in their eating or sleeping habits, or by acting extra fussy or clingy.

In addition, toddlers often have regressive behaviors, meaning they are suddenly unable to do things they previously mastered. They may start wetting their pants or insisting on drinking from a bottle instead of a cup. These are all likely indications that they are feeling insecure about their world. What they need most during this time of uncertainty is comfort and routine.

 Ideas: Supporting Infants and Toddlers

• Offer infants or toddlers extra physical contact. Don't be worried about spoiling them.

• Carry an infant around in a pack close to your body.

• Play games that involve extra physical touch.

• Talk or sing to infants and toddlers in a soothing voice.

• Play calming music in the house.

13

• Maintain their daily routine as much as possible.

• Keep the implementation of new skills to a minimum. If the illness is progressing quickly, it would not be a good idea to try potty training or weaning a young child.

• Accept your children's need to regress. It is their way of returning to an age of safety. It will be temporary, and scolding will not make it go away.

• Try to avoid putting an infant or toddler into a new childcare situation that could create additional insecurities.

Your Child's Friends

Although children instinctively use their friends as a support system, it is common for them to avoid discussion about their sick family member. They may feel embarrassed to bring friends home or may feel ashamed that their family is suddenly different than other families. If their feelings of discomfort get too great, they may withdraw from their friends.

 Ideas: Supporting Your Child

• Although you probably aren't able to tolerate a lot of children around the house, try to find a time when you can encourage your children to have their friends over. They will undoubtedly have questions, and once they feel more knowledgeable about the situation, they may feel less fearful and can then be more supportive to your children.

- Acknowledge to your children and their friends that things are different now. If you can add some humor, (e.g. "How do you like the new bald look?") you will likely put the children at ease.

School

It is helpful for school personnel to be aware of what is happening in your child's life since the illness will undoubtedly affect your child's concentration, academic performance, and relationships with classmates.

However, be sure to include the child's input as to how and when other students should be told about the illness. Well-meaning teachers who announce to the class that a particular student has a very sick family member will likely horrify the child rather than provide needed support.

Most children do not want to be singled out or stigmatized in any way with their peers, regardless of the situation at home.

 Ideas: Support at School

- Take your child with you when you visit the teacher or school counselor so he/she will be fully aware of the information that has been disclosed.

- Make a plan together about how your children will get extra emotional or academic help if needed.

Children Need to be Included

Preparing children to cope with a family crisis starts by including them in the changes that are happening and the decisions that are being made.

Changing Family Routine

Your family routine has probably been altered due to the illness. The changes may be as simple as an occasional medical appointment or as complex as your entire schedule being altered. Your children may not know how they fit into this new routine. Find ways of including them as the routine changes.

 Ideas: Including Children in New Routines

• Let the children choose a job which they alone are responsible for in the care of the ill person. Possibilities could include: reading the paper, giving foot or back massages, serving tea or juice, or decorating the walls with artwork.

• Ask for the children's input regarding new activities your family could enjoy together that involve limited energy or strength.

• Invite the children to join you for an occasional medical appointment. Encourage them to write down questions for the medical provider before they go. Asking questions now can prevent years of misinformation.

- Ask your children for ideas about changes that need to be made in your house to accommodate medical equipment.

- Occasionally allow one child at a time to stay home from school to enjoy the day with the sick family member when he/she is having a good day.

Preparations for Death

Making preparations for death can be tremendously helpful for children and others left behind after the death. Many families lose out on this opportunity because they wait too long and the sick person doesn't have enough energy to participate.

As you and your loved one make preparations for death, think about ways to include the children. Remember, preparing to die does not require the loss of hope or desire to live.

 Ideas: Preparing Children for a Death

- If the ill person is a parent, talk to the children about who will care for them after the death. Children worry about being left without a care provider if something were to happen to the second parent as well.

- If you're planning to use a funeral home, find one that enjoys meeting the needs of children. A discussion with the funeral director and a tour of the building could help your children feel less frightened later.

17

Ideas: For the Sick Family Member

The following suggestions may be emotionally difficult, but they could help a great deal in your children's healing process after you are gone.

• Write a letter to each of your children. Tell them how much you love them and ways in which you are proud of them.

Share memories you cherish and explain things you wish had been different between you.

You can either deliver the letters in person or ask someone to distribute them after you're gone. Your children will then be able to read the letters as often as needed for years to come.

• In the letter you could include information about normal grief:

"If you feel a little relief when I die, it's normal. Don't feel guilty about it."

"If you feel guilt or regret about things that happened between us, that's normal too. However, don't dwell on it – let it go. Guilt will prevent you from healing."

"If you feel angry, don't blame other people or become bitter. Do something positive with your anger energy and it will eventually subside."

- Make movies of normal activities: read a story, play a game, have a conversation or sing a song. Children often worry about forgetting their loved one's voice or facial expressions after a death.

- Have your picture taken with each child doing something you have enjoyed together. Pictures are very precious after the death of someone loved.

- Document your thoughts related to your illness, your life, your struggles, your joys, and your love so your children can feel close to you as they grow up.

- If you have information about special belongings or family heirlooms in your home, make notes about them or they may lose their sentimental value to your children.

- Think of something special you could give each child as a keepsake. Memorabilia, especially things you personally give to them, will be treasured throughout their lives.

- Make something for each child.

- Children often worry a parent won't love them anymore after they die. Assure your children your love will last forever.

- If you have older children who are pulling away from you during this time, tell them it's normal and not to feel bad about it.

Answering Your Child's Questions

Children will likely have many questions, even if they feel uncomfortable asking them. Be honest if you don't have the answers for their questions. Simply tell them that some questions don't have answers.

Keep in mind that when children ask questions, they may really be trying to check out their own thoughts. Ask them what they think about the question before you try to answer it.

Child: *"Why is Daddy sick?"*

Adult: *"Why do you think Daddy is sick?"*

Child: *"Because he caught a bug... I'm never going bug catching again."*

You may learn valuable insights about the thoughts of your children by asking them to answer their own questions.

Finding Meaning

It is often helpful for the person who is terminally ill to know that their life had meaning, even if it is being cut short.

 Ideas: Finding Meaning

- Compile a book of pages contributed by friends and family and give it to your loved one as a gift. The pages could be entitled:

  Thank you for . . .

  Your life has been a gift to me in these ways . . .

One thing I'll always remember about you is . . .

I want to tell you that . . .

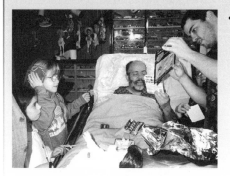

• Have a Celebration of Life party during a time when your ill family member is feeling up to it. Invite friends from all areas of your life and provide a time for sharing comments about ways in which others have been touched by his/her life.

Spiritual Beliefs

If your family has spiritual beliefs, your faith will likely bring comfort and hope to you as well as your children.

Even if your family does not talk about spiritual beliefs, you may find that your children may want to talk about the afterlife or the meaning of death.

 Ideas: Spiritual Beliefs

• Offer your children a visit to a respected religious leader or friend to discuss their spiritual questions. If you need suggestions about which spiritual leaders in your community are comfortable talking about death issues, ask your local hospice or hospital chaplain.

• Be sure you clearly explain the finality of death before concentrating on afterlife explanations or your children may become confused. *"Mommy is going to live with Jesus"* could mean to young children that she will return just like she does when she goes to visit Grandma.

21

• If your religious beliefs include the separation of the spirit from the body, it can be described to children by using a glove and your hand.

Put your hand in the glove and explain that as long as your hand [the spirit] is in the glove [the body], it is able to function properly. When your hand is pulled out, the glove looks the same, but it can no longer function.

• Many spiritual beliefs include miraculous healings. It is my experience that most terminal illnesses lead to death, even with the greatest of faith. Time is precious during a terminal illness and many important things can go unsaid if discussions revolve exclusively around the hope of healing.

Preparing for Visits

If your loved person is in the hospital or does not live in your household, take your children for a visit. Several things to keep in mind:

• Children need to be thoroughly prepared for what they will see. Surprises of medical equipment or changes in appearance can be very disturbing. Explain in detail what special equipment is for and why changes in appearance are happening.

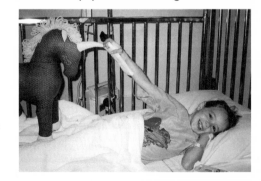

- Remind them that regardless of how the loved person changes in looks, he/she is still the same on the inside.

- Encourage the children to take gifts of art, notes, photos, or flowers, but not food unless you know that patient is hungry for something specific. Appetites are quite unpredictable during a serious illness.

- Allow, but don't require the children to be affectionate with their loved person. Let them do whatever seems comfortable for them.

- Expect young children to make comments that embarrass you such as,

"Aren't you dead yet?"

Don't reprimand them for doing this; they are simply trying to understand what death is about.

- After the visit, talk about how it felt for them. Don't pretend the children didn't notice changes in their loved person.

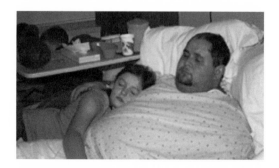

Children Need to Express their Grief

What is Grief?

Grief is the distress we experience when something in our life changes due to a loss. Regardless of the hope for your loved person's recovery at this point, your family has already begun to grieve since news of a life-limiting illness significantly changes your life.

Every member of your family will experience grief in a different way, with a different set of grief symptoms.

It may be difficult to understand how members of your family can grieve so differently from each other. One individual may feel exceptionally anxious or active, wanting to do things, and another may feel constantly fatigued or withdrawn.

The following are some of the more common grief symptoms that children experience during a terminal illness.

Normal Symptoms of Grief

Emotional
Denial
Anger or rage
Guilt or regret
Fears [new or increased]
Anxiety
Numbness
Sadness
Loneliness
Mood swings

Behavioral
Trouble in school
Acting "too good"
Regression [bed-wetting, etc.]
Clingy behavior
Aggression
Irritability

Physical
Stomachaches
Headaches
Fatigue
Appetite changes
Sleep disturbances

Mental
Concentration difficulties
Forgetfulness
Confusion

Social
Increased conflict with others
Withdrawal

Spiritual
Questions about faith,
    meaning, or the afterlife

Expressing Grief

When adults express grief, they generally choose methods that involve words. They may talk about their thoughts or feelings, write about them, or think about them, but all of these involve the language of words.

Young children, however, often have difficulty using words to communicate their inner world. Instead, they generally speak a language that involves the use of behaviors and various forms of art and play.

These allow them to use symbols rather than words. These languages are often so unfamiliar to adults that they don't even recognize them as expressions of grief.

Behaviors

Very young children often express grief by acting clingy or irritable. They seem to require constant attention during a time when adult energy, patience and time is at a minimum.

Older children may exhibit any of the following behavioral patterns when expressing grief:

> Acting out - anger
> Withdrawal
> "Overly Grown Up" behavior

Acting Out

Children who express their grief by acting out are easy to spot and seem to find endless ways of getting into trouble. They may start fights, talk back to adults, refuse to do homework, or explode at the slightest incident.

- Children who speak this language of grief may be expressing a number of feelings that can't be spoken with words.

- They may act out as a way of feeling powerful during a time when they feel quite helpless.

- They may unconsciously feel the illness is their fault, and making people angry with them is a way of punishing themselves.

- They may act out around the ill family member as a way of keeping distance from the painful thought of separation.

- They may simply be creating chaos to describe the chaos they feel inside.

Anger

Perhaps the most common reason kids act out is that they are just plain angry that the terminal illness has disrupted their lives in such a big way.

Anger is normal during a terminal illness and should not be considered wrong or bad. It is the emotion we experience when we feel we have been violated in some way, and a terminal illness certainly violates life as we anticipate it.

Anger is also the emotion we express when we try to hide a variety of other uncomfortable feelings such as guilt, fear or sadness, all of which are normal during this time as well.

Anger itself is not destructive. It is the way we choose to ventilate

anger that determines how negative the outcome will be.

If we give our children the message that it is bad to be angry, they will learn to direct their anger inward which could set them up for depression, feelings of guilt or physical illness.

Our job as adults is to model and teach children appropriate ways of expressing anger that are not hurtful to themselves or others.

Ideas: Expressing Anger

• Acknowledge how difficult this time must be for them.

• Talk together about anger and the many reasons why kids or adults might feel angry during this time.

• Since children who act out often have extra energy, provide them with activities that involve a lot of physical movement.

• Give the children as many choices as possible in their lives to help give them a sense of control.

• If you suspect your child may be feeling responsible for the illness, review the cause of the illness, emphasizing that nothing they did, said, or thought contributed to the terminal illness.

• Make a family list of acceptable ways to express anger at your house that don't hurt self, others or belongings.

Anger activities could include:

Writing in a journal

Expressing anger through art

Running

Doing push-ups

Swimming

Jumping rope

Dancing

Chopping wood

Hammering nails

Stomping around the yard

Punching pillows or punching bags

Throwing ice cubes at trees or fences

Playing loud or calming music

Drumming

Screaming outdoors or in the car

Enjoying a good laugh or a good cry

Talking to a trusted friend or family member

• Talk with your child's teacher or school counselor about ways your child can express anger at school without getting into trouble.

Withdrawal

Withdrawal is another behavioral language children speak when expressing grief. Children fluent in this language may act as if nothing has changed. They don't act out and they generally don't

give much of an indication about how they are doing. In reality, they may actually feel so numb or scared they don't even have words to describe how they're feeling. They tend to get forgotten because they demand so little attention.

Ideas: Withdrawal

• Make an effort to spend time with these children, even if they don't ask for your attention. Go for a walk, shoot some baskets or take a drive so you can be physically close together.

• Don't badger them to talk to you about how they are doing. They may not know and their defenses may be temporarily protecting them from information too painful to absorb. Simply be with them.

• If you know you cannot be available to spend private time with these children for whatever reason, ask a trusted friend to help.

Overly Grown-up Behavior

Children who act "overly grown-up" are often quite pleasant to be around. They are helpful, they try to please others, and they excel in school or extra-curricular activities. Most parents are proud to tell their friends how well their child is handling the family stress.

Children may act "overly grown-up" in an effort to:

• Relieve guilt

• Bargain for more time with the loved person

• "Fix" the family that seems to be falling apart

• Protect the family from additional stress

• Avoid facing the pain of reality

In the long run, the health of these children is at risk. They may develop physical breakdowns when they can no longer maintain their high standards. Eating changes or sleeping disturbances are often the first signs of depression in these kids.

 Ideas: Overly Grown-up Behavior

• Give positive feedback for the expression of negative feelings.

• Don't expect too much from them around the house, even if they appear to be competent at everything they do.

• Encourage them to spend time with their friends, doing activities that were enjoyable for them before the illness.

• Intervene if you hear friends or family encouraging your children to "be strong" or admiring them for doing so well.

• Assure your children that although they may see you cry or display emotions they haven't seen before, they need not feel responsible to take care of you or be strong for you.

Art and Play

The most natural
language children
use to process
their thoughts and
emotions is the
language of art and
play.

Instead of expecting children to talk about their feelings, give them opportunities to express their feelings through art and play. Play allows children the opportunity to bring out feelings at their own pace and in their own safe way.

Using art and play, children will tell their own stories using materials that symbolize how they feel. They will take on different roles in an effort to understand their world.

In one game they may play a helpless victim, and in the next, a hero who conquers evil. Both games can be a child's way of exploring the helplessness he/she may feel.

When children are working through issues about death, they will likely use symbols which represent fear or death in their play.

- They may draw pictures of things that scare them.

- They may include a dead or dying character in their
imaginary games.

• They may draw disturbing pictures of fires, dismembered bodies, ghosts or skeletons.

• If the terminally ill person is a parent, they may start including orphans in their stories.

Regardless of what symbols children use, it is frequently disturbing for adults to watch their children play or draw about fear or death. It is a natural tendency to want to tell kids to play something "nice."

However, this kind of play is normal and healthy and should be encouraged without criticism. The more children can express themselves through symbols, the less control the feelings and fears will have over them.

Although adolescents will probably not use play to express their complex world, they may use various forms of art to disclose their experience. In this way they can express themselves without the terrifying pressure of verbalizing their feelings.

Ideas: Art and Play

- Provide plenty of time to play or draw. Although watching TV for long periods of time may provide you with some needed quiet time, it does not allow time or a helpful setting for children to process their feelings.

- Provide materials needed for art projects or play. If friends ask what they can do for you, suggest they give your children some of the following:

    Art pads, markers, crayons, colored pencils, paints, play dough, clay, puppets, or toy sets that include people.

- Encourage your children to keep an art journal if they enjoy drawing. Suggest writing the date and something about their picture on each page.

- If they have trouble getting started, suggest a few themes and let them choose one that has meaning for them.

    Draw a picture of Dad doing something he enjoys.

    Draw a picture of you and Grandma together.

    Paint a picture of something that makes you mad.

    Mold something out of clay that looks like Mom's sickness.

    Draw a picture of somebody who is scared.

    Paint a picture of something you wish you and Grandpa could do together.

Although you will learn a lot from their art or games, avoid interpreting what you see.

You may think you see an angel in the sky that is protecting the house below when, in actuality, it might be a death ghost that has come to take the entire family away. If you say, *"What a nice angel,"* the child may become confused and shut down.

If you want to learn more about their artwork, simply ask, *"Would you like to tell me about your picture?"* This gives the child the option of saying "*no,*" and it leaves all of the interpretation up to the child.

Over time you may notice recurring themes in your children's art or play. This may give you a glimpse of the things they are struggling with or the areas in which they need more education from you.

What Children Need During the Days Surrounding the Death

You may be part of a culture that is rich with traditions and rituals around death. On the other hand, if you're like many families, your experience with death or death rituals may be very limited. Preparing children for these events involves giving them information about what to expect and allowing them to participate in the process as they choose.

Comfort Treatment

When it's time to make the decision to switch from life-saving treatment to comfort treatment, explain your decision to the children or they may feel confused or angry that nobody is calling 911 when their loved one is in pain or becoming unresponsive.

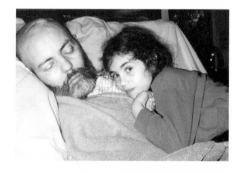

Approaching Death

The final stages of life can be confusing or frightening for children if they don't understand why things are happening. Not all terminally ill people experience these common changes, but the following are conditions your children may benefit from discussing.

Loss of Strength

At the end of life, the disease may weaken the body so much that your loved one may need to rest almost continuously. Eventually he or she may be unable to talk or even open his or her eyes.

Even at that point, however, he or she can still hear your voice and feel your touch. Most people appreciate their loved ones talking to them, even if they can't respond.

Loss of Appetite

It is normal for terminally ill people to lose their appetite slowly until they may not be able to eat anything at all. Children need to know that their loved person's body can't tolerate normal amounts or certain types of food anymore. It is important to allow the sick person to eat what he/she tolerates without being pressured to eat more.

Pain or Discomfort

Many diseases cause pain or other uncomfortable symptoms. There are many medications these days that can be used to relieve most levels of pain or discomfort. Assure the children the medical provider and hospice nurses will do all they can to keep your loved person comfortable.

Personality Changes

Some people experience a change in personality as their body weakens. Someone who normally has a level temperament may suddenly get frequent crying spells or angry outbursts. Your children need to know the disease is influencing these changes.

Confusion

Some diseases cause confusion toward the end of life that can be very frightening for children. If your family member starts saying or doing things that don't make sense, discuss it right away. Don't pretend the children won't notice and don't assume they will understand that the sick person is confused.

Breathing Changes

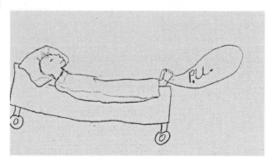

It is common during the last few days or weeks of life for a person's breathing patterns to change.

The breathing may sound loud and heavy, there may be pauses between breaths, or it may sound like your loved one needs to clear his/her throat. Explain that these breathing patterns are much like snoring - they're uncomfortable to listen to, but the person doing them is unaware of how they sound.

The Death

Although many adults feel that children should not be present at the death of a loved one, it could be a very positive experience for your children. The transition from life to death is generally more peaceful than anticipated and witnessing this moment firsthand can give children a sense of reality.

However, first consider how you, the child's role model, are feeling about being present at the moment of death. If you are afraid you will become hysterical when the death occurs, you will likely frighten your children. However, if you are feeling at ease about being present, invite them to join you but leave the decision up to the child. Never force a child to unwillingly be present.

Of course, many people die when their family members are out of the room and the choice of being present is not an option. Considering this, never promise yourself or your children to be present at the moment of death.

Many people who work with the terminally ill believe that people close to death somehow know when it's time to slip away. Some seem to wait until every last family member has arrived, and others seem to wait until everyone has stepped out of the room, as if they want to slip away unnoticed. Assure children they don't need to feel frightened if they are present, or guilty if they aren't present, at the moment of death.

When death is close at hand, think about ways of making the transition from life to death as smooth and comfortable as possible for them. Keep in mind that your loved person will likely be more aware of his/her surroundings than it appears.

Ideas: As Death Approaches

- Play some favorite music.

- Read a favorite or comforting passage from the Bible or another book.

- Tell stories about memories that come to your mind.

- Touch him/her in comforting ways.

- Give him/her permission to go. It is important for your loved one to know you no longer expect him/her to keep fighting.

- When your loved one finally stops breathing, give yourselves permission to feel some relief. It is very normal and does not indicate a lack of love or sadness.

Gone From My Sight

I am standing upon the seashore.
A ship at my side spreads her white sails
    to the morning breeze and
    starts for the blue ocean.
She is an object of beauty and strength.

I stand and watch her until at length
    she hangs like a speck of white cloud
    just where the sea and sky come
    to mingle with each other.

Then someone at my side says,
    "There she goes!"

"Gone where?"

Gone from my sight... that is all.
She is just as large in mast and hull and spar
    as she was when she left my side and
    she is just as able to bear her load of
    living freight to the place of destination.

Her diminished size is in me, not in her.
And just at the moment when someone at my side says,
    "There she goes!"

There are other eyes watching her coming, and
    other voices ready to take up the glad shout,
    "Here she comes!"

And that is dying.

- Henry Van Dyke

After the Death

Resist the temptation to rush your loved one's body away before the children wake up or arrive home. It is usually very helpful for them to see their loved one after he/she has died. There may be other friends or family who would be grateful for an invitation to join you before you call the mortuary.

 Ideas: After the Death

- Offer everyone a chance to spend time alone with your loved person. There may be things that need to be said that were too difficult to say while he/she was alive.

- Let the kids climb on the bed or do whatever seems comfortable. Young children may want to snuggle up to their loved person or they may need to examine the body for missing parts.

- Children of any age may want to check for signs of life. If so, encourage them to check for breathing or listen for a heartbeat.

- Say some prayers.

- Light a candle. You could buy a candle large enough to burn continuously from the time of death until the memorial service.

- Give a toast in celebration of your loved one's life.

- Invite friends and family to share memories.

When everyone is ready, call the mortuary. When they arrive, you may want to ask them to leave your loved one's face uncovered so you can all say good-bye.

The Days Between the Death and the Death Rituals

During the days following the death, you will probably be very busy making decisions, talking on the phone, or visiting with guests. Some children love this increased level of activity and others feel lost with all the extra commotion.

Find time to spend with your children even if you need to leave the house to avoid interruptions.

 Ideas: Days Following the Death

- Explain in detail what the children can expect to happen during these days.

- Decorate a table with flowers, candles and pictures of your loved one. If he/she died at home, you could place the table in the room where the bed was.

- Decide together what clothing or personal items should be taken to the funeral home to be placed in the casket.

- Make a secret family list of "Crazy Things People Say After Someone Dies." This gives the children something to do with well-meaning but uncomfortable things they may hear.

- Laugh together about funny things that happen or stories people tell about your loved one. Laughing can be very healing.

- Let the children help answer the phone or keep a log of thoughtful things others do for your family.

- Make a plan for what to say if someone calls asking for your loved one. It can be very upsetting if children are caught unprepared.

- Talk about whether or not you'd like to change the message on your answering machine if it includes the voice of the person who died.

The Death Rituals

Children generally have no idea what happens at death rituals. Describing each event in detail beforehand will help ease their anxiety.

Viewing the Body

Even if you are planning a cremation, provide children an opportunity to see their loved one's body. Children have imaginative minds and may picture the dead body without a head (because we say, "s/he can't see or hear anymore"), or without arms or legs (because we say, "wash your arms, your legs, and your body").

Seeing the body will correct their distorted images and help them positively identify their loved one. Some children have dreams for years that the mortuary got the wrong person if they never got to see their loved person with their own eyes after the death.

Young children may talk in a loud voice in an attempt to awaken their loved person.

They may imagine they see their loved person breathing. It is important to look with them, without criticism, until they are convinced they were mistaken.

Children are naturally curious and may want to touch, poke or push on the body to see how it feels. This exploration should be accepted, but never force a child to touch or kiss the body.

Ideas: Death Rituals

• Ask a funeral director to be available to talk to the children if they have any questions related to the funeral home process.

• Put a stool close to the casket so young children can look inside again and again without help.

• Show children the whole body. Some assume the lower half has been cut off if it is covered in a casket.

• Provide permanent markers and encourage guests to sign the casket.

• Leave a basket of pens and index cards in the viewing room and invite guests to write a good-bye note to place in the casket.

• Leave markers and art paper for children who prefer to express their thoughts in a drawing.

The Funeral/Memorial Service

The purpose of a funeral or memorial service is to give friends and relatives a chance to face the reality of death and to reflect on the life of a loved one in an atmosphere of love and support. Children of all ages should be given the opportunity to attend this significant event if they so choose.

Memorial services can be emotionally painful, but keeping children away does not prevent them from experiencing the pain of grief. It simply gives them the message that they are being excluded from something important. This often results in feelings of isolation, confusion or resentment.

If the details of the service are explained to children ahead of time, it is likely they will only benefit from observing the ritual and the grief of those who cared for their loved person.

There are many ways to include children in the planning of a service.

 Ideas: Funeral/memorial Service

• They could make a photo display of your loved one.

 • They could help chose items to display that represent the life of your loved one. Things such as handmade items, jewelry, favorite objects or familiar pieces of clothing could be included.

• Children could help choose photographs or video clips to include in the production of a short movie or slideshow about your loved person.

• They could decorate the church or meeting place with artwork about their loved one.

- Children could make a list of things they love about the person who died and one of them could read it aloud during the service.

- They could read a poem they've written or a children's book about unending love (see Recommended Resources).

- They could sing a song, play an instrument, make some comments or pass out programs.

- You could ask a friend or the minister/priest to do a children's story as part of the service.

- Large index cards could be passed out for the guests to write down a favorite memory, a funny story or a word of appreciation about your loved person. The children could then read them again and again as they grow older.

- Have paper and markers available for kids to use during the service. They may not cry or act like they're listening, but they will probably draw about what they're hearing or feeling.

- Video-recording the service would allow young children, or children who chose not to attend the service, to view it later. This is especially helpful for young children who may want to watch the service again when they get older.

- If your children don't sit with you at the service, make sure they sit with someone who is willing to spend time explaining things to them and answering their questions.

- You could even let the children plan a service of their own, allowing them to invite whomever they'd like and do whatever they find meaningful.

The Burial

We often think of a burial service as the time to release a body back to the earth. However, the opportunity to do this is completely avoided if we neatly hide the hole beneath the casket so it isn't even visible, or we leave the casket sitting above the ground until everyone is gone. Young children can actually leave the cemetery without understanding that the body of their loved one is going to be buried there.

This confusion can be avoided by simply allowing them to see with their own eyes what will happen to the casket. Be sure to remind young children that your loved person no longer feels anything so being buried will not hurt him/her in any way.

Ideas: The Burial

- Let the children help carry the casket.

- Show them the hole in which the casket will be placed.

- Allow them to watch the casket being lowered into the ground.

• Bring shovels and offer the children a chance to help cover the casket with dirt.

• Pass out markers and helium balloons and invite children or adults to write notes on them. Release them as a symbol of letting go.

Cremation

Adults often worry that children will be horrified if they learn their loved one will be cremated. In actuality, if your words and your tone convey that you are comfortable with the process of cremation, your children will likely feel the same way, especially if you explain the reason it was chosen.

Explain that when bodies are buried, they break down over the years until only a skeleton remains. Cremation is just a way of making that process happen much faster.

Young children are often curious about the cremation process. They may want to know what the crematorium looks like, what kind of container the body will be in, and how hot the oven will get. They may even want to see or touch the ashes.

Many adults do not know much about cremation, so learning about it will make it easier to describe it to children in simplified terms.

Explain that a crematorium is a small steel room that gets about three times as hot as your oven can get at home. The body is placed in a sturdy cardboard container or a casket, it is slid into the cremation chamber and the heat is turned on. It gets so hot that in

2-3 hours, only about 5-8 pounds of coarse sand-like ash remains if the person was an adult.

The family then decides what kind of container they would like to put the ashes in. This container is often called an urn.

Remind young children that cremation will not hurt.

If your children would like to see or touch the remains, allow them to do so after you prepare them by describing what they will see.

Following the cremation include the children in the decision about what to do with the ashes. You have infinite choices about where to distribute them, and you have plenty of time to decide. This can be a very healing process if you don't rush into it. Many families wait for months or even years to make the decision.

Ideas: Cremation

• You could have the ashes buried in a cemetery and mark the spot with a special grave marker. This may be especially important to you if there are other loved ones buried there.

• You may want to plant a new tree or bush in a nearby park and distribute some ashes around its base. This would give you a chance to watch the tree grow and mature, as you will, over time.

• You could brainstorm together about your loved person's favorite places or places you enjoyed as a family. These could include anything from a shopping mall to a favorite hiking trail. Then figure out how to discreetly place some ashes in one or more of those locations.

• Consider putting at least some of the ashes in an accessible place close to your home for those who need a specific place to go to grieve their loss. But remember, if you put them in your yard and you move away at some point, you will no longer have access to that spot.

Returning to School

Children will have a variety of responses to the thought of returning to school following the death. Young children may be anxious to get

back to school to tell everyone about the death while older children will likely dread the thought of returning to school.

Friends and school staff are rarely comfortable in knowing how to deal with a bereaved child. Many will either ignore the subject of the death or they will give the child too much attention, both of which are extremely uncomfortable for the returning student.

Ideas: Returning to School

• Together with the teacher, give your children a few choices about how they would like their return to be handled in their classroom. Some children will want to tell their classmates about the death or memorial service and others will not.

• Often the class has already heard about the death and classmates will have questions for your children when they return. They may want to rehearse responses to possible questions.

• Older children often dread attention related to the death, yet they feel uncared-for if nothing is said about their significant loss. Talk about how their friends and teachers react and discuss which approaches are most helpful.

• Explain to the children that some things people say in an effort to be comforting actually feel hurtful. Encourage them to focus on the intention of the words rather than the words themselves if this happens.

- Continue your family list of "Crazy Things People Say or Do After Someone Dies." Laughing is a great way to heal from hurtful comments.

- Give the children a small item, like a smooth rock or a personal belonging of your loved one, to put in their pocket. When they start to feel sad or worried, they can reach for the item and rub it to relieve their anxiety.

- Talk to the school counselor or principal to make sure there are understanding people available to talk to when needed.

- Teenagers may need your help in talking with teachers about catching up on school work. Some teachers may allow alternate assignments to be done in place of the original ones (e.g. rather than the missing English assignment, a paper could be written about the person who died).

What Children Need to Heal from their Loss

Healing from a significant death is a process that spans over a lifetime. The pain of the loss, however, decreases over time provided the children have adequate support throughout the grieving process.

Grieving children need to:

Acknowledge their Loss

Embrace Memories

Feel and Express the Pain of Loss

Integrate the Death into their Lives

Children Need to Acknowledge their Loss

Before children can grieve the loss of someone loved, it is necessary for them to confront the reality that someone significant has died and will not be returning.

Even though your children may have known your loved one was going to die, it might still come as a surprise to them, especially if they were accustomed to a lot of ups and downs during the illness.

It may take several months for them to acknowledge the death. If the illness was a recent diagnosis or information was distorted or withheld from them along the way, it may take even longer.

If you haven't already done so, provide the children with a meaningful way of saying good-bye to your loved one.

 Ideas: Acknowledging Loss

- Write a good-bye note on: a biodegradable helium balloon and watch it float away, on a piece of wood and let it float down a river, or in a bottle and send it out to sea.

- Write a good-bye letter or poem.

- Make a good-bye gift and keep it or give it away.

- Draw a good-bye picture.

- Compose a good-bye song and sing it at the grave site.

- Go to the cemetery or a special place and tell the loved one good-bye.

Children Need to Embrace Memories

Acknowledging the death does not mean the relationship with the loved person is over. Healing involves the development of a new relationship that is based on memory rather than presence.

Some cultures have meaningful traditions that include when and how to remember and honor the person who has died.

However, many do not and children may get subtle messages that it's best to forget the person who has died and move on. This is communicated when adults avoid talking about their own memories. Some households even have an unspoken rule that the loved person is never to be mentioned again.

This may seem like the easiest way to get on with your lives, but the long term results can be devastating to the children's physical and mental well-being. The only way for children to find hope and healing is by embracing their memories.

 Ideas: Embracing Memories

• Talk freely about memories, even if it brings tears.

• Create a Facebook page or an online memorial so friends and family who are scattered can share memories and stay connected.

• Let the children pick out keepsakes from your loved one's belongings. If the children are quite young, save some things to give them when they get older.

• Make a scrapbook or picture collage of your loved person.

• Get prints made of your children's favorite photos of the loved one so they can keep them in their room.

• Get the children an art pad, journal or workbook to record memories.

• Hang a graffiti board in the house entitled "Things I Miss About _____ ." Let each family member contribute to the board as they wish.

• Read children's books about remembering loved ones who have died [See Recommended Resources.]

• Ask friends and relatives to talk about their memories.

• Make a quilt for each child out of the loved one's clothing.

• Visit places of special significance.

• Find a special place to plant a tree or some bulbs in memory of your loved person.

• Talk about or draw the dreams you have of your loved person, even if they don't make sense.

In addition to good memories, your children probably also have some unpleasant memories of the person who died. These memories will also need to be embraced and shared in order for healing to take place.

60

Assure your children that it's normal to remember unpleasant things after someone dies and give them permission to share those memories with you or another support person.

If memories include those of physical, sexual or emotional abuse, professional help may be needed before your children will be able to mourn their loss.

Holidays and Other Special Days

Bereaved families experience a great deal of distress around the holidays, the anniversary of the loved person's death and other significant days of the year.

Some families valiantly attempt to celebrate these special days as if the loss never happened. Although tension is high and there is an obvious hole without the loved one, the subject of the loved one is never mentioned. This rule of silence is quickly learned by the children and often results in many years of strained family gatherings.

Other families cancel holidays or special days completely, resulting in great loneliness as each family member is left alone in their grief. Children are particularly disturbed by the loss of family traditions in addition to losing the person who died.

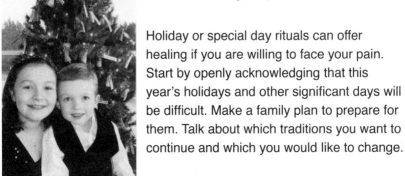

Holiday or special day rituals can offer healing if you are willing to face your pain. Start by openly acknowledging that this year's holidays and other significant days will be difficult. Make a family plan to prepare for them. Talk about which traditions you want to continue and which you would like to change.

61

Build into your plans specific ways of honoring the memories of your loved person on special days. The children need to know that the significance of their loved one did not end with his/her death.

 Ideas: Holidays and Other Special Days

• Look at photo albums or home videos from years past.

• Visit the grave site to plant bulbs or have a picnic.

• Take a trip you wish you could have taken together.

• Take flowers or cookies to a place your loved one worked or volunteered.

• Give a gift to an organization your loved person cared about.

• Spend the day doing random or deliberate acts of kindness.

• Request your loved one's favorite song on the radio.

• Have a potluck gathering of friends who helped your family through the illness and death.

• Buy a card or gift to encourage someone.

• Pass out art materials and invite everyone to draw a picture of their favorite holiday memories.

- Make a collage of their favorite holiday photographs.

- Return to a previous vacation spot.

- Have your loved one's jewelry altered or made into new pieces for you or your children.

- Buy a special memorial candle to light on each significant day.

- Declare the anniversary of the death a family holiday and spend the day doing things your loved person enjoyed.

- If it was a mom who died, keep in mind that young children often make projects in school for Mother's Day. Plan ahead for what your children will do during this difficult time.

- Plant a memorial flower garden.

- Treat yourselves to a box of extra soft tissues for the tears that may naturally flow on these significant days.

Children Need to Feel and Express the Pain of Loss

"Time does not heal a painful loss...
Grieving does."

-Anonymous

We often want to believe that time alone will provide healing following a significant death. We quickly move the children away from uncomfortable feelings, and we keep ourselves busy to avoid facing the pain of loss. However, it is moving *toward* the pain of grief that ultimately heals.

Children express pain differently at various ages and at different stages of the grieving process. Their reactions also depend on who died, how long the individual had been sick, and how prepared they were for the death.

The following are some generalizations about how children of various ages react to death and express the pain of loss. Please keep in mind that what works with one child may not work with another.

Age 0-2

Toddlers often initially express feelings of loss by looking repeatedly for the person who died. They may look in a familiar spot or in the place the loved one was last seen.

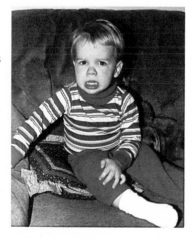

If they are able to talk, they may ask for the person over and over. They may scream or act angry in an effort to bring their loved person back.

Eventually the toddler will give up hoping for the loved one's return and sadness will set in. The child may become temporarily uninterested in food, toys or activities.

Regressive behaviors may be noted. The child may temporarily stop talking or go back to crawling.

Children of this young age can have lasting vulnerabilities to separation and loss if support is not given.

 Ideas for ages 0-2: Expressing Pain

• Provide physical comfort. It may not immediately ease the pain of separation, but it will eventually facilitate healing.

• Accept the child's regression without criticism.

• Give the child a piece of clothing that still has the loved person's smell on it.

• Give the child a picture of their loved person to carry around.

• Make up a photo album from extra pictures of your loved one and keep it in a place that is accessible to the child.

Age 2-6

Parents often perceive children at this age as being relatively unaffected by the death. They may go play shortly after hearing the news of the death and they rarely cry at first. They may act as if they aren't grieving at all.

They may do or say things that seem inappropriate to adults.

At some point they start displaying behavior changes such as increased anger, regression or clingy behavior.

They often have new or increased fears and nightmares for some time after the death.

At this age children are not able to understand abstract concepts like heaven. They may picture it as a bunch of dead bodies laying all over the ground or a place like jail where people are forced to stay against their will.

The concept of "forever" is also too abstract. They may ask if they can write a letter to their loved one to beg him/her to come home, as if he/she could choose to come back.

Since they believe in magical thinking, they may think they have caused the death in some way, even if they observed the entire illness and dying process.

Once these children realize their loved person is not coming back, they may yearn for him/her to the point that it makes adults feel desperate to relieve their child's pain.

Children in this age group move toward pain primarily by using art and play. They may turn the couch into a casket, they may pretend someone has died, or they may draw angels and caskets or other death symbols. This is very healthy and should be encouraged.

Ideas for ages 2-6: Expressing Pain

• If your family talks about heaven, encourage your children to draw pictures of what it must look like so you can get a glimpse of the images they have in their minds.

• Give positive comments about your child's death play and art and make suggestions for further exploration.

• Be patient as you repeat information about death's permanence.

• Set limits for inappropriate behavior and accept your children's regression.

• Provide comfort when your children have nightmares and encourage them to draw their dreams if they remember them the next morning.

Age 7-11

By this age, children have a much greater understanding of the future and therefore what the loss will mean to them.

Even though they yearn for the person who has died, they often hide their tears because they don't want to appear childish or helpless.

They don't want to be different in any way from their peers, and they are very sensitive to teasing about the death from other children.

67

Because they're aware that they too could die, these children may become fearful of sleep or darkness, or they may worry that their own aches and pains could lead to death.

They may try to hold on to their loved one by adapting his/her behaviors or mannerisms. Photos and objects that belonged to the person who died are particularly important for children of this age.

They have a well-developed capacity for feelings of guilt and they often have regrets about things they did or didn't do before the death, especially if the loved one was a sibling.

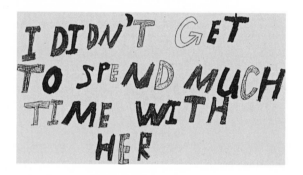

Although children in this age group are more capable of language, they tend to express their grief in art, stories, music, play and behaviors.

Often, aggression problems develop in school, especially for boys this age. There may also be regressive, withdrawn or overly grown-up behaviors.

 Ideas for ages 7-11: Expressing Pain

• Encourage keeping a journal, drawing pictures, or writing stories, poems or music about their feelings or experiences.

• Allow for the release of energy through physical activity.

• Take them to a bereavement support group for children their age.

• Set limits for aggression and accept regressive behaviors.

• Model and encourage the expression of a range of emotions.

• Create ways to release feelings of guilt.

• Write letters to the person who died.

• Work with the school staff about academic problems.

• Help educate your children's friends about how to be supportive.

• Offer reading materials to be read alone or together [see Recommended Resources].

Teens

Teenagers may feel they need to be strong so they can care for the rest of the family. Their pain tends to express itself through physical symptoms, depression and anger.

They will likely be moody and they may become bossy in an effort to appear powerful and in control.

They frequently express anxiety about the death by being reckless with their own lives to show they are not vulnerable to death. They may drive at high speeds or abuse drugs or alcohol.

Girls may increase sexual activity in an attempt to receive physical comfort. Boys may seek body contact and tension relief by fighting or becoming aggressive.

There are often problems with dropping grades in school, even if the death was expected for quite some time.

This can be a very confusing time for teens as they struggle to become independent from their parents, yet suddenly find themselves feeling helpless and dependent.

Unlike the younger ages, teens often express their feelings of grief through language. They may feel, however, that emotional expression is not acceptable to their friends.

Occasionally teens may feel that in order to honor the individual who died, they should quit using a skill they learned from that person. Tremendous gifts can be lost when teens quit playing a musical instrument or stop doing creative projects in an effort to honor the person who died.

Ideas for Teens: Expressing Pain

- Talk about ways to honor someone who has died. Invite friends from various cultures to talk about their traditions.

- Talk about options other than drugs or alcohol to deal with the pain of grief.

- Look for artwork, music or writings other teens have written to express their grief.

- Give your teen a camera for capturing images that represent their grief.

- Watch for reckless or impulsive behaviors.

- Set limits but don't become too controlling.

- Offer books about teen grief or purchase a teen grief workbook for their own private use.

- Be available to them and encourage getting support from others as well.

- Teens often feel alone in their grief. Consider taking them to an adolescent bereavement support group in your community. There they will discover that their feelings are normal, they are not alone, and they will learn valuable coping ideas from other adolescents their age.

- Consider attending a support group of your own. The more comfortable you feel with your own grief, the more you can be of help to your teenager.

Children Need to Integrate the Death into their Lives

The death of a family member forever changes a child's understanding of the world. Healing requires that the child find meaning in the death, develop a new self-identity and reinvest his/ her emotional energy into other relationships.

Search for Meaning

Whenever we lose something dear to us, we are also given an opportunity to find things in our lives we wouldn't have otherwise found. After the death of a loved one, the grief path seems to split, creating a choice that needs to be made about which path to follow.

One path circles around and around, staying focused on the pain of loss and the unfairness of the death. The other path moves forward, always searching for the gifts that can result from painful experiences.

Jasmine Pearson

This search for positive meaning can take years, but it often results in a wisdom about life that can be gained only when one experiences a great loss.

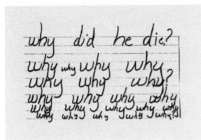

You will be your child's role model as they choose which path they will take. If you become resentful about the loss and begin circling around, your children will likely follow.

On the other hand, if you begin looking for positive meaning in your life as a result of the death, your children will likely begin struggling to gain personal growth as well.

New Self-identity

Children often understand themselves in terms of their relationships with others in their lives. They may think of themselves primarily as a younger brother or "Daddy's little girl." Thus when someone in the family dies, they must reestablish who they are without the loved person.

Many children experience regressive behaviors during their quest to discover their new self-identity. This is a very normal way for children to express their need for support and safety. As your child heals, the need for regressive behaviors will lessen.

After a death, children must also redefine their roles in the family. Jobs that used to be done by the person who died must now be distributed among the remaining family members. Children often describe this as being a very difficult adjustment.

Be careful not to expect too much from your children. They should not be expected to act like grown-ups, nor should they be encouraged to be "the man or woman of the house." Allow them to grieve normally for their age.

If possible, wait for a while before moving, changing childcare situations or selling family possessions. It will be much easier for children to adjust to one change at a time.

Reinvesting Emotional Energy

If children experience a great deal of pain with their loss, they may be afraid to love anyone again. They may even feel that developing new relationships would be disrespectful to the person who died.

As your children learn to adjust to the death of your loved one, they will learn to reinvest their emotional energy in new relationships and learn to love again.

Childhood Traumatic Grief

Most children experience normal grief after the death of someone loved. However, occasionally a child will get "stuck" thinking about the way the person died and they aren't able to get beyond those thoughts to start working on the normal tasks of grieving. This could happen if the child perceives the death to be shocking, unexpected or horrifying in some way.

During traumatic grief children are unable to think about memories of their loved one without their mind being drawn back to the image they have of the terrible death. Since these thoughts are frightening,

the child may try to avoid thinking about the person who died all together. Of course, they can't stop thinking about their loved one, so even happy memories will lead to upsetting or terrifying thoughts.

Signs that a child may be experiencing traumatic grief may be noticeable shortly after the death or it may take months or even a year for it to become apparent. Although some of these symptoms are normal for any grieving child, they should not persist over time.

Signs to watch for:

- Intrusive memories or comments about the terrible death
- Avoidance of friends, family or reminders of the person who died
- Teens may start or increase their alcohol/drug use
- Physical or emotional symptoms:

Irritability or anger
Trouble sleeping
Decreased concentration
  with a drop in grades
Physical complaints
  without medical findings
Fears about safety for
  oneself or others.

If you have questions about whether or not your child may need professional help, don't hesitate to ask your school counselor, medical provider, or local hospice or counseling center for advice.

Conclusion

Grief varies in length and intensity depending on one's personality, available support, the magnitude of the loss, and the history of other losses in one's life.

As your children grow and reach new developmental stages, they will re-grieve their loss again and again as they reach new levels of understanding. This is very normal and should not cause concern.

They will need your continued support throughout their lives as they discover new meaning related to the changes they have experienced during the grieving process.

Blessings to you and your family as you continue your journey through grief.

Grieving is not weakness

Nor absence of faith.

Grieving is as natural as

Crying when you are hurt,

Sleeping when you are tired or

Sneezing when your nose itches.

It is nature's way

Of healing a broken heart.

- Doug Manning

Recommended Resources

PICTURE BOOKS – *Recommended for all ages*

Badger's Parting Gifts. Varley, S. ~Memories.

Butterfly Kisses and Wishes on Wings. McVicker, E. ~Someone loved has cancer.

Buzzy Jellison: The Funeral Home Cat. White, A. ~Funeral home.

Daddy's Chair. Lanton, S. ~Dad death: Jewish culture.

Everett Anderson's Goodbye. Clifton, L. ~Dad death.

Goodbye Boat. Joslin, M. ~Saying goodbye.

Gran-Gran's Best Trick. Holden, L. D., ~Grandpa illness and death.

Grandma's Shoes. Hathorn, L. ~Memories of grandma.

How Can I Help, Papa? Al-Chokhachy, E. ~Grandpa illness and death.

I Miss You: A First Look at Death. Thomas, P. ~General information about death and grief for very young children.

Lifetimes: The beautiful way to explain death to children. Mellonie B. & Ingpen, R. ~The life and death of plants, animals and people.

Old Pig. Wild, M. ~Grandma prepares to die.

Saying Goodbye to Lulu. Demas, C. ~Pet death and healing from loss.

Someone I Love is Sick. McCue, K. ~Parent & grandparent versions. Cancer & death for very young children.

Tear Soup: A Recipe For Healing After Loss. Schwiebert, P. & DeKlyen, C. ~Healing after loss.

The Dream Jar. Johnson, L. L. ~Turning bad dreams into good dreams.

The Empty Place. Temes, R. ~Sister dies of a terminal illness.

The Invisible String. Karst, P. ~Connected by love.

The Next Place. Hanson, W. ~Afterlife.

The Two Of Them. Aliki. ~Grandpa death.

There's No Such Thing As A Dragon. Kent, J. ~Impact of denial.

Too Far Away to Touch. Newman, L. ~Uncle illness and death from AIDS.

Tough Boris. Fox, M. ~It's OK to cry.

Waterbugs & Dragonflies. Stickney, D. ~Explaining death to young children.

What is Heaven Like? Lewis, B. ~Christian beliefs about death.

When Dinosaurs Die. Brown, L. & Brown, M. ~Death and grief.

When Someone Dies. Greenlee, S. ~General grief.

Wherever You Are My Love Will Find You. Tillman, N. ~Love endures.

CHAPTER BOOKS - Fiction

A Ring of Endless Light. L'Engle, M. ~Grandfather death.

A Summer to Die. Lowry, L. ~Sibling death.

Alex: The Life of a Child. Deford, F. ~Sibling death.

Mama's Going To Buy You A Mockingbird. Little, J. ~Dad death.

Sadako and the Thousand Paper Cranes. Coerr, E. ~Friend death.

The House Without A Christmas Tree. Rock, G. ~Holiday memories.

With You and Without You. Martin, A. ~Dad illness & death.

You Shouldn't Have to Say Good-bye. Hermes, P. ~Mom death.

CHAPTER BOOKS – Non - Fiction

How It Feels When A Parent Dies. Krementz, J.

Learning to Say Good-bye. LeShan, E.

Lost & Found: A Kid's Book For Living Through Loss. Gellman, M. & Hartman, T.

Our Mom Has Cancer. Ackerman, A.

TEENS

Chill and Spill Journal. Lorig, S. & Jacobs, J.

Fire In My Heart-Ice In My Veins: A Journal For Teenagers Experiencing A Loss. Traisman, E. S.

Healing Your Grieving Heart for Teens: 100 Practical Ideas. Wolfelt, A.

I Will Remember You: A Guidebook Through Grief for Teens. Dower, L.

Just One Tear. Mahon, K. L. ~Teen diary about a dad's death.

Part of Me Died, Too. Fry, V. L.

Saying Goodbye When You Don't Want To: Teens Dealing With Loss. Bolton, M.

Teenagers Face to Face with Bereavement. Gravelle,K. et al.

When a Friend Dies. Gootman, M.

PARENTS

A Decembered Grief. Smith, H. I. ~Ideas for holidays.

Final Gifts: Understanding the Special Awareness, Needs and Communications of the Dying. Callanan, M. & Kelley, P.

Guiding Your Child Through Grief. Emswiler, M.A. & Emswiler, J.

How To Help Children Through a Parent's Serious Illness. McCue, K.

Keys to Helping Children Deal With Death and Grief. Johnson, J.

Talking About Death: A Dialogue Between Parent and Child. Grollman, E. A.

The Power of Your Child's Imagination. Reznick, C.

Understanding and Supporting a Child or Teen Coping with a Death. Cameron, J. B.

When a Parent Has Cancer. Harpham, W. S.

ONLINE RESOURCES

Centering Corporation (centering.org) – A grief resource center.

Compassion Books (compassionbooks.com) – A grief resource center.

Compassionate Friends (compassionatefriends.org) – Support after the death of a child.

GriefNet.org – Online grief support.

Grieving.com – Online grief support.

Kidsaid.com – Online grief support for kids.

National Alliance for Grieving Children (childrengrieve.org) – Information about needs of grieving children.

National Child Traumatic Stress Network (nctsn.org) – Information about child trauma.

National Hospice and Palliative Care Organization (nhpco.org) – Find a hospice near you.

New Day Foundation for Families (foundationforfamilies.com) – Hope, healing and resources for families of young children who lose a parent to cancer.

The Sibling Connection (counselingstlouis.net) – A resource for anyone who has lost a sibling.

Book Order Information

Preparing the Children

*Information and Ideas for
Families Facing Serious Illness and Death*

~ a publication of ~

Gifts of Hope

For ordering information
find us on our website:

preparingthechildren.net

For questions
contact us at:

preparingthechildren@ak.net